J 796.2
WOO
Wood, Tim
Skateboarding

$10.40

DATE DUE		
DE 21 '89		
NOV 1 7 '9		
JL 22 '9		
JL 27 '9		
AN 25 '97		
JL 29 '9		
MY 04 '0		
JE 27 '0		
JE 25 '02		
AG 19 '0		
MR 01 '0		
SE 25 '04		
NO 0		

MY SPORT
SKATEBOARDING

Tim Wood

Photographs: Bob Pickett

Franklin Watts
London • New York • Sydney • Toronto

© 1989 Franklin Watts

Franklin Watts
387 Park Avenue South
New York
NY 10016

Phototypeset by Lineage, Watford
Printed in Italy
Designed by: K and Co

ISBN: 0-531-10830-9
Library of Congress No: 89-50203

Illustrations: Simon Roulestone

The publishers, author and photographer would
like to thank Wurzel, and Jeremy Fox of
Deathbox Skateboards for their help and
cooperation in the production of this book.

A message from Wurzel:
**When you start skateboarding or when you are
learning new tricks, make sure that you wear
the proper safety equipment. This should
include a helmet, gloves, and protectors for your
elbows and knees.**

The skateboarder featured in this book is Wurzel. He is twenty-five years old. His father bought him a small fiberglass skateboard when he was twelve and he has been hooked on the sport ever since. Wurzel spends up to six hours each day skating. He loves the sensation of speed, the challenge of learning new tricks and the feeling of being half out of control! Wurzel is a member of the Deathbox Skateboard Team. He turned professional in 1987 and has skated in the United States and in many European countries. He now writes for skateboard magazines, gives skating demonstrations and performs in skateboarding videos. He also has his own signature model skateboard.

I am a skateboarder. Today I am taking part
in the first National Streetstyle Skateboard
Contest in Britain. I arrive at the
skateboard park in the morning and wait with the
4 other skateboarders to go in.

When I get into the park, I check over my skateboard. I make sure that the plastic railbars are fixed tightly to the bottom of the deck.

The top of the skateboard deck has a roughened surface which helps my feet grip it. I use a special key to tighten the screws which join the trucks to the deck.

The bottom of the deck is painted with my own graphics. I use the angled kick-tail at the back of the deck as a lever to raise the nose of the board. It soon loses its paint as it scrapes along the ground.

More about skateboarding

There are three main styles of skateboarding:

Freestyle, where the skateboarder skates over a flat, smooth surface, performing tricks on or with the skateboard.

Streetstyle, where the skateboarder skates over obstacles, performing tricks on the skateboard.

Ramp skating, where the skateboarder skates backwards and forwards on a half-pipe ramp performing stunts at the highest point of his or her run. These are called "lip-tricks" because they are tricks performed on the lip, or top edge, of the ramp.

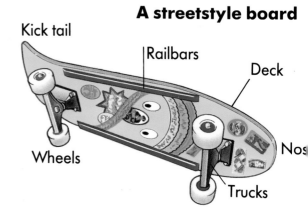

A streetstyle board

Kick tail

Railbars

Deck

Nos

Wheels

Trucks

The deck curves up at the edges
Graphics decorate the bottom of the deck

Some skaters prefer straightforward **downhill racing** or **slalom,** which is racing downhill while weaving through a twisting course made from plastic cones.

Freestyle

Streetstyle

Ramp skating

8

Some obstacles which may be used in a streetstyle skating contest:

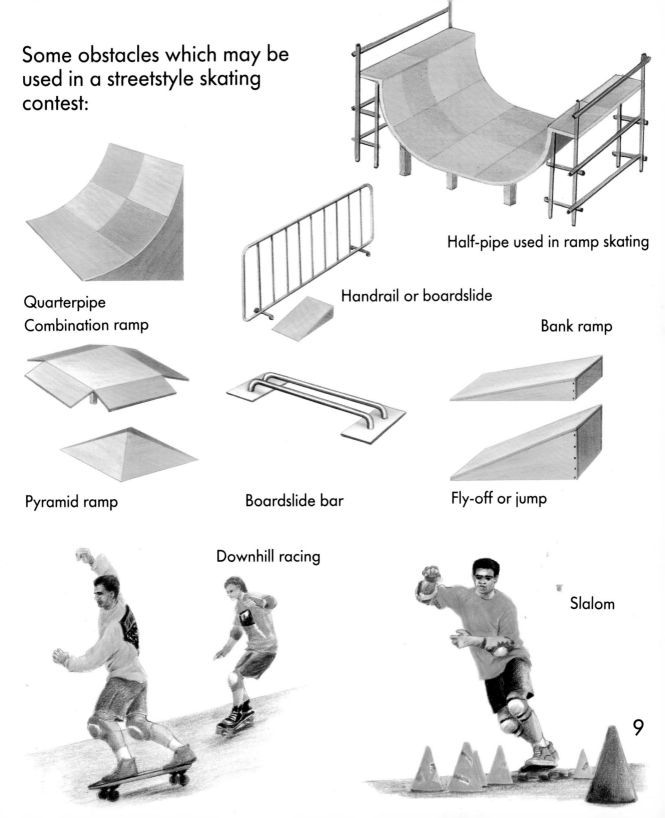

Half-pipe used in ramp skating

Quarterpipe
Combination ramp

Handrail or boardslide

Bank ramp

Pyramid ramp

Boardslide bar

Fly-off or jump

Downhill racing

Slalom

9

Part of the skateboard park has been laid out
for the Championships with ramps and other
obstacles. I join the other skaters for a
practice session.

As I skate around, I put up stickers that advertise the skateboard company that sponsors me. My sponsors hope I will do well so that people will buy their skateboards and skateboarding products.

Streetstyle skaters do tricks while riding over various obstacles. This one is called a combination ramp. I use my speed and the slope of the ramp to take off so I can perform an aerial trick, or "air."

No-handed aerials like this "Ollie" need a
lot of practice to do correctly.

One of the most difficult obstacles on the course is an old car. I try out a few tricks as I skate over the roof. Here I am "bailing" or falling off!

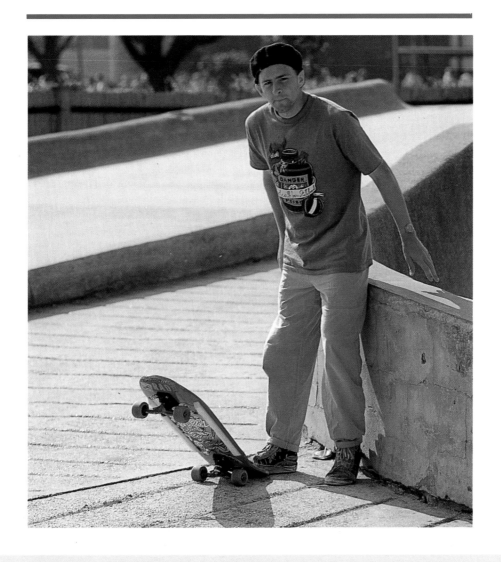

After a while, I leave the main arena and move to one of the smaller practice areas or "bowls." Skaters perform in these bowls one at a time. I wait at the side for a chance to take my turn, or "snake."

15

Once a skater has snaked, he or she has the right to skate alone in the bowl. Skaters can continue to skate until they fall off or decide to leave the bowl. The other skaters wait their turn to snake while the performance goes on.

I use the edge of the concrete ramp to do a "rock and roll slide." I balance the skateboard across the concrete rim while it slides along the rim on its railbars.

Parts of the bowl are steeply banked. I skate down one side and then use my speed to skate along the banking to perform a "kick turn."

You need a good sense of balance and fine timing to perform difficult aerials. I push down on the kick-tail to lift the board and then push down with my front foot on the deck to make it "stick" to my feet for this Ollie.

There is a half-pipe in the park for ramp skating. The skaters build up a tremendous speed going down the wall and then use this to help them perform stunts like these "lip-tricks" at the top of the other wall.

This skater is trying to perform a "backside invert." BMX riders and rollerskaters also use the big half-pipe to perform tricks.

I am not a ramp skater, but streetstyle
skaters can use anything to help them perform
their tricks. I skate onto the half-pipe just
long enough to do an Ollie off it.

This skateboarder wants my autograph. I sign the bottom of his deck.

The competition begins in the early afternoon. I join the audience to watch the first skaters perform. Everyone groans very loudly when a skater falls off. They bang their skateboards instead of clapping.

Now I take my turn. Each skater is allowed about one minute and fifteen seconds to perform. Skaters are marked for their skill and for the variety of tricks they do.

I try to skate as smoothly as I can, but also include some difficult tricks. This is a

"method air" on the combination ramp.

I build up my speed as I skate towards the
car. Getting over it is harder now that other
skaters have knocked out the windows.

27

The contest is over. I did not win, but winning is not important to me. Skateboarding is not as competitive as other sports. I skate to improve my skills

and to entertain the audience.

As I skate to the station, I see a wall that no streetstyle skater could resist! I have just enough time for a few more wall rides before I catch my train.

Facts about skateboarding

Skateboarding was invented in the United States. It was very popular about ten years ago, then nearly died out. It has recently become popular again.

Skateboarding was made possible by two inventions, both of which were first used on rollerskates and then later adapted for skateboards. The first was the skateboard truck which is springloaded so the rider can tip the deck to one side. This makes the wheels turn and so steers the board. The second invention was polyurethane roller wheels. These are not only much quieter than earlier wheels, but also have low-friction bearings which allow them to keep turning for much longer.

Skateboarders move along in three main ways. The first method is "pushing," where a skater balances on the board on one foot and pushes along with the other. The second method, called "pumping," is where the skater stands with both feet on the board and moves the board by bending his or her knees and twisting his or her body in a rhythmic motion. The third method is to build up speed by skating down a slope.

The best skateboards are made from Canadian maple wood. This material is flexible enough to allow the board to twist and bend, but strong enough to withstand the shocks of heavy landings and fast changes of direction. Other materials like fiberglass and graphite are usually too heavy or too expensive.

GLOSSARY

Aerial
A trick performed in mid-air. Also called an air.

Deck
The flat body of the skateboard.

Graphics
Designs painted on the bottom of the deck.

Kick-tail
The curved back end of the skateboard.

Lip-trick
A trick performed by ramp skaters at the top edge of a half-pipe ramp.

Low friction bearings
Smooth running wheel hubs.

Ollie
An aerial trick in which the board "sticks" to the skater's feet without any help from the hands.

Railbars
Plastic runners on the underside of the deck.

Rock and roll slide
A sideways slide on the railbars on the top edge of a half-pipe.

Signature model skateboard
A skateboard that is named after a famous skateboarder.

Snake
To take a turn skating.

Sponsor
A company that supplies a skater's equipment in return for that skater wearing the sponsor's advertising on his or her clothes and equipment.

Trucks
The turning mechanism used on skateboards.

31

Index